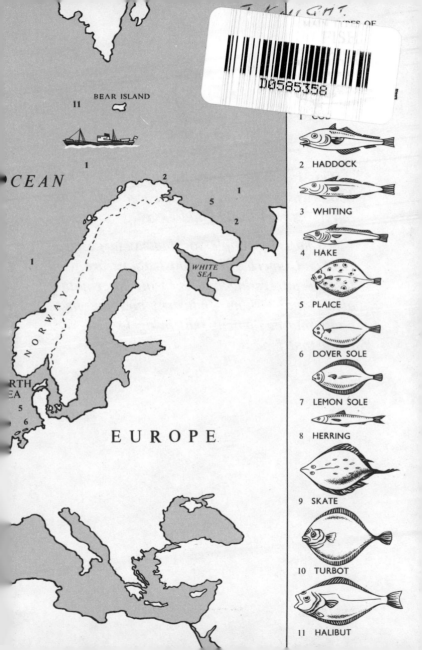

BEAR ISLAND

11

1

CEAN

2

1

5

2

WHITE
SEA

1

NORWAY

RTH
EA

5

6

EUROPE

1 COD

2 HADDOCK

3 WHITING

4 HAKE

5 PLAICE

6 DOVER SOLE

7 LEMON SOLE

8 HERRING

9 SKATE

10 TURBOT

11 HALIBUT

Series 606B

This is another carefully planned Ladybird book which will help to answer the many questions that lively children ask.

A relatively simple vocabulary, large clear type and superb colour illustrations are used to give interesting and accurate information about the Fishing Industry, and the men, boats and equipment that bring us this very important food.

'People at work'
THE
FISHERMAN

by I. & J. HAVENHAND
with illustrations by JOHN BERRY

Publishers: Ladybird Books Ltd . Loughborough
© Ladybird Books Ltd (formerly Wills & Hepworth Ltd) 1963
Printed in England

The life of a fisherman is a hard one. He spends most of his time at sea in all kinds of weather.

He wears special clothes to keep him warm and dry. When it is wet and stormy the fisherman wears an oilskin macintosh. His hat is made of oilskin, too, and is called a sou' wester. The long sea-boots a fisherman wears reach right to the top of his legs.

A fisherman always carries a good clasp-knife. He uses this knife to clean fish and mend nets.

7214 0065 5

Fishermen go to sea in many kinds of boats. They use different kinds of nets to catch the fish which are all shapes and sizes.

Small boats are used for fishing near the shore. These are not large enough to go very far from land. Inshore fishermen catch their fish and return home every day.

The larger fishing boats are called trawlers and drifters. These boats can stay at sea for a long time and the fishermen live and sleep in them.

Inshore fishermen often catch lobsters and crabs. They use pots or creels for this. A lobster pot is made of basketwork, and looks like a cage with a hole in the top. This hole is made in such a way that the lobster or crab can get in but cannot get out.

A piece of fish is put in the pot as a bait. Each pot has a line fixed to it with a float on the other end. This is so that the fisherman can see where his pots are.

Fishermen in trawlers catch such fish as cod, haddock, whiting, hake, and flat fish like halibut, plaice and sole. These fish are called demersal fish and live near the sea-bed.

Some of these fish are still caught by hooks on long-lines. These long-lines can have up to five thousand baited hooks on them and are laid on the sea-bed. Fishermen use long-lines where the rocky sea-bed would damage the trawl-nets.

To-day most demersal fish are caught by trawlers.

COD

HADDOCK

PLAICE

DOVER SOLE

TURBOT

WHITING

RED MULLET

SKATE

The largest trawlers are called distant-water trawlers and come into such ports as Hull, Grimsby and Fleetwood. They have a crew of about twenty men.

Distant-water trawlers stay at sea for three weeks or more. They travel up to three hundred miles a day to reach the fishing grounds near Greenland, Bear Island and the White Sea. These fishing grounds are over one thousand, five hundred miles from port.

These fishermen mainly catch cod. The seas are very cold and codfish like to live in colder waters.

The home ports of middle-water trawlers are Grimsby, Fleetwood and Aberdeen.

Middle-water trawlers are not as large as distant-water trawlers. There are about fifteen men in the crew and they stay at sea for about two weeks. They travel to fishing grounds in the North Sea, the Faroe Islands and Iceland. These fishing grounds are between two hundred miles and one thousand miles from port.

The fishermen catch all kinds of fish, but mainly flat fish such as halibut, plaice and skate.

The smallest trawlers are called near-water trawlers. They use Grimsby, Fleetwood, Aberdeen and Milford Haven mainly as their home ports.

Near-water trawlers have a crew of about ten men, and stay at sea for almost a week. Fishermen in near-water trawlers do not go to the colder fishing grounds. Their fishing grounds are the North Sea and the warmer, shallower waters around our coasts.

The fish they catch are hake and flat fish such as plaice, turbot and sole.

A man called the ship's husband looks after the trawler while it is in port.

It is his job to see that the trawler is fitted out for each trip.

There must be enough food and fresh water on board the larger trawlers to last at least three weeks.

The fuel tanks must be full and the engines, winches and ropes checked.

Powdered ice is taken into the holds. The fish are packed in this as soon as they are caught.

Fishermen in all three kinds of trawlers use trawl-nets. A trawl-net is like a big bag which is dragged (or trawled) on the sea-bed. The net is about one hundred and fifty feet long and the mouth, or open end, is about eighty feet wide.

When the trawl-net is down, the bottom of the mouth drags along the sea-bed on rollers. The top is kept up by floats. The sides of the mouth are kept open by boards called otter-boards.

The trawler pulls the trawl-net along by cables from the two otter-boards.

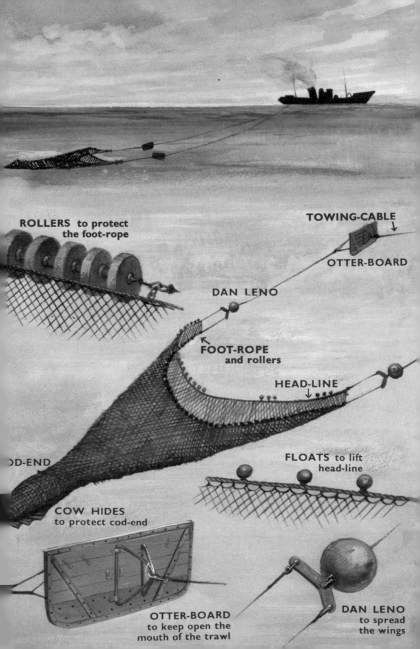

ROLLERS to protect the foot-rope

TOWING-CABLE

OTTER-BOARD

DAN LENO

FOOT-ROPE and rollers

HEAD-LINE

COD-END

FLOATS to lift head-line

COW HIDES to protect cod-end

OTTER-BOARD to keep open the mouth of the trawl

DAN LENO to spread the wings

When the fishermen put the net into the sea they call it 'shooting the trawl'.

The trawler stops and all the fishermen stand by the side of the ship. They push the big net over the side and use the winch or crane to lift the metal floats over. The heavy rollers go over next and the net begins to sink. The otter-boards follow and the towing cable is let out.

When enough cable is run out it is fixed to the stern and the trawler begins to move.

As the trawler drags the net along the sea-bed the fish are swept into it through the mouth. They cannot swim out again because inside the mouth is a funnel of fine net. This is called the fish trap. The closed end of the net is called the cod-end.

When the trawler is towing the trawl, the fishermen fix a fish basket to the mast to warn other boats.

The fishermen use an instrument called a fish-detector. This tells them when there are plenty of fish near the net.

The fish detector works by sending a sound to the bottom of the sea. This sound always comes back to the ship. If any fish get in the way of this sound-wave, the sound bounces back more quickly to the detector.

On the bridge is a glass-fronted box. In this is a moving roll of paper with a pen-nib almost touching it. The detector is set so that the pen marks the paper when it passes over fish. When there are a lot of fish the mark is thicker.

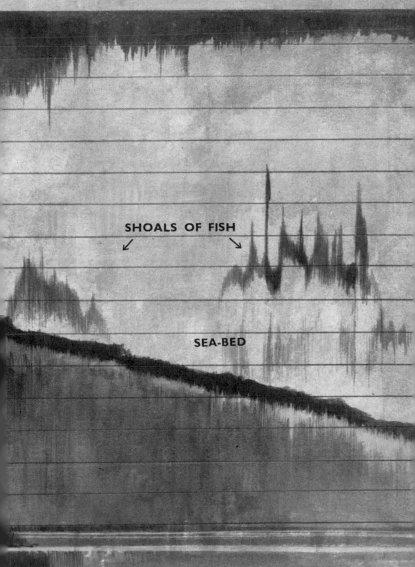

SURFACE

SHOALS OF FISH

SEA-BED

When it is time to haul in the trawl-net the skipper calls all hands on deck.

The trawler is stopped and the winch starts to pull in the net. The otter-boards come up first and then the rollers and floats.

The fishermen grip the net and drag it on board. As soon as all the net is on board the mate pulls loose the cod-line. When this rope is pulled the cod-end of the net opens.

As the net opens the fish come falling and slipping out on to the deck. The fishermen look at the catch to see if it is a good one.

When the net is empty the cod-line is tied again. The trawl is shot and trawling carries on.

The fishermen now begin to clean the catch. This is called gutting the fish. They cut each fish open with a sharp knife and take out its inside. The liver is saved and is used to make cod-liver oil.

The gutted fish are thrown into a long, narrow tank. In this tank they are washed with water from a hose-pipe. This is to make them clean so that they will keep.

When the fish have been washed they are put into the hold of the trawler. A layer of fish is put on some powdered ice. The fish are then covered with more ice. This is done until each part of the hold is packed with layers of fish and ice.

The fish will now keep until the trawler reaches port.

The skipper decides when it is time to return to port. He tells the radio-operator to send a message to the trawler company. In the message he tells them how big the catch is and when he expects to reach port.

As soon as the boat ties up in the fish-docks the fishermen's job is over. They say good-bye to the skipper and go home for a few days.

Fish-handlers now go on board the trawler to sort and unload the fish ready for market.

Some fishermen go to sea in boats called drifters. Drifters are about half as big as trawlers and often they stay at sea for only a day or two.

Fishermen in drifters catch fish that live nearer the top of the sea. These fish, such as herrings and mackerel, are called pelagic fish.

Drifters usually go to sea in the afternoon. They travel to the fishing-grounds about fifty miles away. The fishermen are then ready to shoot the nets in the evening.

Drift-nets are different from trawl-nets because they are not made up like a bag.

A drift-net is just a large sheet of netting. This hangs down in the water with weights on the bottom and floats on the top. A rope leads from the net to the drifter. Each net is about one hundred and fifty feet long and fifty feet deep. Sometimes up to a hundred of these nets are joined together. They hang in the sea like a net wall and stretch for over a mile.

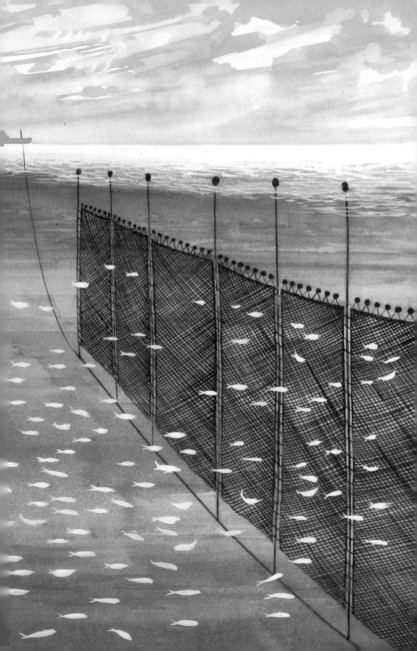

Fishermen in drifters use nets with different sized mesh or holes to catch different kinds of fish.

The shoals of fish try to pass through the floating nets. They swim into the nets and can get their heads through. The fish cannot get back because they are caught in the nets by the gills.

When the nets are shot one of the fishermen stops the engine of the drifter. The nets and the boat just drift in the sea. This is how drifters get their name.

At dawn the fishermen haul in the nets. This is hard work as the nets are heavy with water and thousands of fish. The fishermen use a capstan to help them.

They shake the fish into the holds and pack away the nets. The drifter then races back to port for the catch to be sold.

Some of the herrings are sold to be eaten fresh. Others go to be smoked and turned into kippers in kilns (as shown). Some go to the factories to be cooked and canned.

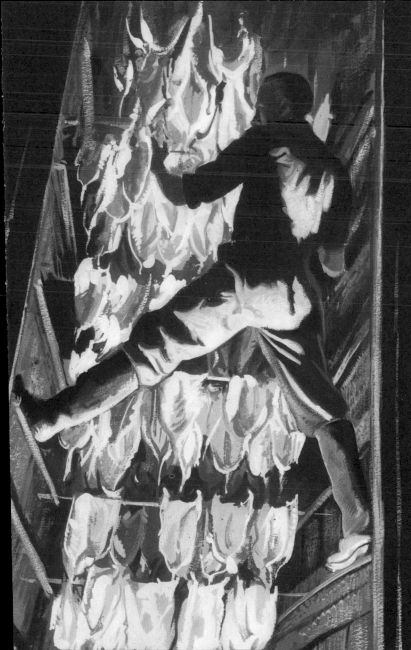

Some fishermen go to sea to catch whales. To do this they have to travel to the colder waters of the great Antarctic Ocean in the southern part of the world.

Whales are not really fish, but they live in the sea. They are very big and can weigh as much as one hundred tons.

In a whaling fleet there are large factory ships and smaller boats called whalers. The men on the whalers kill the whales. Men in the factory ships flense (or cut up) the whales.

Each whaler has a harpoon gun fixed in the bows. This gun is on a swivel and can be turned all ways. When the harpoonist sees a whale he shoots a harpoon at it. The harpoon is like a spear with a bomb in the end. This bomb explodes and quickly kills the whale.

The harpoon has a rope on it. The fishermen pull the dead whale alongside and pump air into it to make it float. They put a flag on it and then look for other whales.

The men on the factory ships see the flags and collect the whales. They winch the whales on board up a ramp at the back of the ship.

The whale is then cut up on the flensing deck and the meat is frozen or salted.

Other things we get from whales are hides, whalebone, ivory, ambergris for making perfume, and different kinds of whale oil.

The fishermen are away from home for a long time as the whaling season lasts about eight months.

Fishermen all over the world catch other kinds of fish as well.

Two kinds are usually sent to factories to be put in cans. These are sardines and salmon.

Sardines are caught by the million in nets with a small mesh. The most important fishing grounds for sardines are off the coasts of Morocco and Portugal.

Salmon are caught near the mouths of rivers in special nets. Most of the canned salmon that we eat is caught off the west coast of Canada.

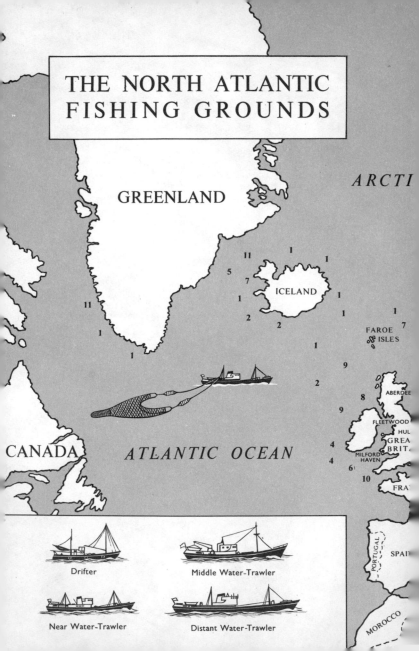

THE NORTH ATLANTIC FISHING GROUNDS

ARCTI

GREENLAND

ICELAND

FAROE
ISLES

CANADA

ATLANTIC OCEAN

ABERDEE

FLEETWOOD

HUL
GREA
BRIT

MILFORD
HAVEN

FRA

PORTUGAL SPAI

MOROCCO

Drifter

Middle Water-Trawler

Near Water-Trawler

Distant Water-Trawler